FAMOUS AMERICAN INDIAN LEADERS

FOREST WARRIOR
The story of Pontiac

Written by: Jill C. Wheeler
Edited by: Paul J. Deegan

1

Published by Abdo & Daughters, 6537 Cecilia Circle, Bloomington, Minnesota 55435

Library bound edition distributed by Rockbottom Books, Pentagon Tower, P.O. Box 36036, Minneapolis, Minnesota 55435

Library of Congress Number: 89-084910   ISBN: 0-939179-69-5

Cover Illustrated by:Liz Dodson
Illustrations by: Liz Dodson

Pontiac dipped his finger in the icy water of the river and let it slice an arrow through the crisp waves. It was a chilly spring morning in 1724. He and his family were gliding through the water in their birch bark canoe on the way to the French traders' settlement near Lake Ontario. His father's strong arms kept up a steady swoosh-swoosh as they flew past the wooded banks on either side.

The 10-year-old Ottawa (AHT uh wuh) Indian boy was excited. This was his first trip to see the French. He had heard many stories about them, and he had helped his father trap the beaver, mink, and otter whose furs they would trade for knives and cloth. Now he would finally get to meet these strange light-skinned people about whom he had heard so much..

His finger was getting numb in the frigid water, so he withdrew it and jammed it inside his deerskin jacket. The long winter was over, but it was still cool. He could hardly wait until he could put aside his leggins and coat and run in just a buckskin breechclout and moccasins.

He nestled down in the furs tucked into a corner of the canoe. One of the finest furs was a mink he

3

had trapped himself. He fell asleep dreaming of the fine French knife for which he would trade when they got to the settlement.

The settlement was bustling with activity when Pontiac and his family arrived. The boy helped his father drag their canoe out of the frigid waters and carry it to the collection of buildings that made up the village. His mother and sister had unloaded the furs and the few provisions each had brought with them. They always traveled light on this journey so they could take plenty of goods back with them after they had bartered with the French.

Most of the activities were taking place in a central meeting hall. Pontiac and his family followed the noise to a large log building. It was very different from the bark-covered building in which Pontiac lived. His house was long and narrow, with many partitions dividing the sleeping quarters of the 10 families who lived there.

Young Pontiac and his family glide through the water in their birch bark canoe.

Inside the meeting hall the air was warm and smoky. There was a fireplace, too, not like Pontiac's house where fires were built under large holes in the roof. The Indian boy looked up to see that the rafters were bare. In his home, the rafters were hung thickly with dried pumpkin strips, corn and fruit. Pontiac wondered briefly if these light-skinned people ever needed to eat.

The log walls vibrated with the hum of many languages mixing together. Pontiac recognized some Indian friends of his father, but he could only stare in wonder at the light-skinned people.

The French traders were bundled in strange clothes. Every part of them was covered. Many of them also had thick, curly hair on their faces. Some, he noticed, carried the terrible fire sticks his father had told him about. One was making strange sounds with a round wooden box which had a long stem on one end.

Pontiac was fascinated by the box. He edged closer to see what spirits were inside it to make it sound as it did.

"You like the fiddle?"

Pontiac turned to see a young French boy smiling at him. He gestured toward the musical box and asked again, "The fiddle? Do you like to hear the music it makes?"

Pontiac was surprised to find a light-skinned boy his own age speaking to him in the Ottawa's language. As if reading Pontiac's mind, the boy continued.

"Yes, I speak Algonkian," the boy said. "My father is a trapper and I learned it from him. My name is Jacques (ZHAHK). By what name are you called?"

"I am Pontiac," he replied. "I, too, am a trapper."

"I am honored to meet you," Jacques said, his brown eyes sparkling. "Since you just arrived, you must be hungry. There is plenty of succotash and venison. We will have lots of time later to talk about trapping. Now we can eat!"

Pontiac and Jacques became best friends during the next three days. The French boy showed Pontiac how to throw knives at targets, and Pontiac taught his new friend how to make a wooden bow for hunting.

One day their fathers and the other adults were busy bartering furs. The two boys snuck out of the meeting house to go hunting. Jacques had his new bow. Pontiac had the knife Jacques had given him. They tramped though the woods for hours. But they did not find any game except for a few squirrels. Pontiac did, however, find a maple tree. He showed Jacques how to tap into its trunk to get the thick, sweet sap.

"Tell me about your home," Jacques said quietly as they sat underneath the tree, sucking the dark sap from their fingers.

"My home is the forest," Pontiac replied. "It gives us shelter, food, clothing, everything we need."

"But you must live in a particular part of the forest, don't you?" Jacques asked.

"No, it is all our home."

"But don't you own part of it?"

"Own the land?" Pontiac asked in surprise. "No one can own the land. Mother Earth is a gift of the Great Spirit. It is here for us to share, not to own."

"Back home in France, we own land," Jacques said.

Pontiac and Jacques talk about their homes.

"The land belongs to your people," Pontiac said, turning to him. "My people belong to the land."

Jacques was silent for a moment, then he began to rise to his feet, gesturing toward the settlement. "It is time to return. Did you not say your family was leaving today?"

"Yes," Pontiac said as he jumped up. "I hope we will meet again."

"You can be sure of that," Jacques said, playfully tugging Pontiac's glossy black braid. "We are brothers now."

For several years afterward, Jacques and Pontiac saw each other at the gathering the traders held each spring. Both began to look forward to meeting and trading stories. Jacques told about life at the settlement. Pontiac talked about his training to become a medicine man.

Pontiac now was in his 20s and had become a member of the Grand Medicine Society. The Society had four steps, or degrees. Members had to attain these steps to become skilled at healing the sick. For each step, Pontiac had to memorize many prayers and rituals. Each spring, there was a special gathering. There, he and the other Society members had a chance to show off their skills. Through the rest of the year, they used their skills to heal others. They did this through their knowledge of plants' healing properties.

Members of the Society also concentrated on learning to communicate with Manitou (MAN i too). This was the great power responsible for the forces of the earth.

One day, Pontiac journeyed to the home of a Delaware Indian medicine man. The man was said to be able to talk with Manitou.

"Manitou has spoken to me," the old man said , his voice raspy and quiet. "His sorrows are many. He sees his children living like the whites, hunting with fire sticks rather than the bows and arrows he has given them. He sees them clothed in the goods of the whites, not the warm skins and furs of his forest creatures. His children are doomed lest they turn away from the whites and live as in ages past.

"He has sent me a vision," the medicine man had continued. "It is a vision of the red coated ones invading the lands he has set aside for us. They are coming to kill. They are coming to take what is no one's to give."

The old Delaware then looked directly at Pontiac. "Go. Tell your brothers that it is time to return to the old ways. They must drive the red-coated ones back to the land the Manitou has provided for them."

Pontiac rose slowly to his feet and moved toward the door of the wigwam. His heart was heavy, for he knew he had much work ahead of him.

Pontiac bent his head into the wind and paddled. Jacques was only a few feet behind him. His friend was catching up to him as the canoe race neared its end.

The tall white cedar tree they had designated as the finish line was only yards in front of him. The year was 1743 and Pontiac was nearly 30 years old. His body was getting too old for racing, he thought.If he could keep the lead!

Pontiac and Jacques have a canoe race.

Whoosh, whoosh, whoosh, went the oars as they cut through the cool river water.

Three more strokes, two more, one more, there! Pontiac had won the canoe race!

He lay back in the canoe to rest. It was a beautiful summer afternoon, the perfect kind for a friendly contest.

"So you won again, but this time I was closer." Jacques was behind him, laughing. "Maybe in another 15 years I will be able to beat you. Then I'll be an old man, too!"

The two guided their canoes to the shore and pulled them up near the cedar tree. They stepped out and plopped down in its shade.

"What is it you say about the white cedar?" Jacques asked. "Something about a boy?"

Pontiac smiled and began to tell him the story of the great Manitou Menabozho.

A small boy once dared Menabozho to do whatever the boy did. The boy put his great toe in his mouth, but Menabozho was unable to copy him. He told the boy he could make any wish, and the Manitou would make it come true. The boy wished for a long life, and Menabozho turned him into a white cedar. He stood that way for many years. It was a reminder that it is not good to be smarter than Manitou.

Jacques laughed out loud again. "And the English, can your Manitou turn them into a forest of cedars? Then they will not bother us again."

Suddenly the air was split by a gunshot. The two friends jumped to their feet and strained their ears to hear more. More shots were fired, and they seemed to be coming from near Jacques' village.

Pontiac and Jacques raced to the edge of the forest clearing where the settlement stood. There, outside the tall walls surrounding the village, they saw a group of Indians. The Indians' fire sticks were aimed at the French fort.

"Iroquois," Pontiac said. "The English have enlisted them to help. We must wait here until nightfall. When it is dark we will sneak back inside and help defend the village."

Shortly after night fell, the two men made their way back to the village. They slept little that night, instead loading rifles and making plans with the other villagers to defend the settlement. When dawn came, bringing with it another attack, they were ready.

The two friends did not know they had witnessed the first battle of King George's War. The war was between the French and the English and their Indian allies. It was named for King George II of England.

Pontiac and his people stood by the French throughout the five-year war. The Ottawas were willing to shed the blood of their Indian brothers to help the French. The French were their brothers in trade.

The battle at the fort was the first of many for Pontiac and Jacques. They had the advantage of knowing the country, but the English had many soldiers, and new ones seemed to appear as fast as the French and Indians could kill them.

One July day in 1755 Indian scouts brought word of the approach of a large group of English soldiers. The soldiers were being led by General Braddock. They were headed for the French Fort Dusquesne (doo KAYN), located in what is now Pennsylvania.

The second in command at the fort was Daniel de Beaujeu (boo ZHOH). He quickly began planning a surprise attack in a nearby bend of the Monagahela (mun NAHN guh HEE luh) River. The soldiers were following the river as they journeyed toward the fort.

Pontiac and his followers joined Beaujeu in the march to the bend where the attack was to occur. All together, they had nearly 850 men. The English, the scouts had said, had nearly 1,500.

Pontiac hoped to catch up to Beaujeu, who was several yards ahead of him.

Suddenly Beaujeu stopped short. He was dressed in all respects as an Indian except for the French tri-corner hat. In an instant he had torn the hat from his head and was whirling it over his head and shouting. Pontiac strained to hear his words, but they were swallowed up in a burst of gunfire. The English!

Pontiac and other Indians dived into the cover of the woods and began to shoot at the red-coated soldiers. The English soldiers fell like dead trees in a strong wind.

The battle raged on for nearly two hours. When it ended, the clearing was littered with dead soldiers, while those who stayed standing raced back the way they had come. They left behind all of their wagons, their supplies and more than 900 killed or wounded. Only a few French and Indian fighters had been lost.

"Where did they come from?" General Braddock wheezed as the defeated troops rolled back toward Virginia. The crimson blossom on the elderly man's chest continued to grow where it had been pierced by an Indian bullet.

George Washington rubbed the general's hand as their wagon rumbled along through the forest. Washington was a young soldier fighting with the English army. He, too, was silent, thinking of the ferocity of the battle they had just escaped. The French and Indians were a force to be reckoned with, the young Virginian thought to himself.

Pontiac attacks fort Detroit.

The enemy had been led by a tall, muscular Indian. He had feathers in his shiny black hair and wore silver bracelets. The leader seemed to have some magical power over his forces. How else would they do his bidding facing such incredible odds?

The war was theirs for now. But their time was coming. That much he knew.

Jacques finished stuffing the last of his furs into a knapsack. Pontiac had given it to him as a farewell gift. The Frenchman was leaving for his homeland. He did not wish to remain in America under English rule. Only a few days before, the Union Jack had been hoisted over Fort Detroit. This signaled the end of French rule in the northern woods.

"I am sad to see you go," Pontiac said solemnly. "You will be missed."

"It is I who is sad," Jacques said. "I am sad that this is your home and you cannot leave it. Already I have seen how the English treat your people.

They are stingy in their trade and they wish only the land, not the bounty it can provide.

"I wish you luck, my brother," he continued. "We French fought and you fought at our side. But it will take more than that to rid the land of the English. May Manitou smile upon you."

Jacques hefted the bulging sack to his shoulder and placed his hand on the door of the log cabin. "I will listen for news of how your battle goes," he said quietly. "If you need me, I will be back."

Pontiac watched his childhood friend trudge through the snow toward the river where his canoe was waiting. As he watched Jacques walk away, a firm resolve grew in the pit of his stomach. He would battle the English like never before, and he would not quit until he had driven them from the land of his people.

He took a deep breath and stepped outside. The war would come, but first he must prepare for it. He would begin by traveling to many villages and telling them about the vision of the Delaware. Then he would inspect the English forts to find their weaknesses. Only then would he attack.

21

"General Gladwin? That Indian Pontiac is here again."

Major Gladwin looked up from his paperwork, annoyed. It was May of 1763 and the weather finally was beginning to get warm. He didn't like the climate at Fort Detroit, much prefering the milder temperatures of his native England. But an English officer had little choice these days.

"What does he want now?" Gladwin asked the clerk. "He was here just a few weeks ago. He probably would have scalped us all then except that Chippewa girl told us to beware. Don't tell me he's going to try to kill us again?"

"I don't know, sir," the young man replied. "He says he wants a friendship council, he wants to smoke the peace pipe with you. He said if you refuse he will throw away the wampum belt you gave him as a token of friendship."

Gladwin grunted. "Those silly Indians and their wampum belts. Why do they tack so much importance on to a string of brightly colored beads?"

"Oh, all right. Tell him he and his people can come in — but only in small groups."

The clerk left, and the Major rose from his desk to watch out his window. He saw the clerk address the tall, muscular chief at the gates to the Fort. He could tell Pontiac was angry with the reply, and the chief and his followers quickly stomped away.

"Good riddance," Gladwin said to himself. "I wish we could just kill them all. They're nothing but trouble."

Later that evening, Gladwin heard drums throbbing faintly in the distance. He walked outside his cabin and listened through the fort's walls. Slowly, he recognized the sound as the Ottawa's war song.

The next day, he received word that nine English settlers had been killed. Pontiac's war had begun.

"You say the savages have jeopardized Fort Detroit?" said General Sir Jeffrey Amherst to his aide-de-camp, Captain James Dalyell. "I find it hard to believe they would have the intelligence to conduct a raid on one of our forts."

"Sir, Major Gladwin reports that the Indians would not be attacking were it not for the chief Pontiac," Dalyell said. "He evidently is behind it all."

"Ah yes, Pontiac. Can we not send those Indians a load of blankets from small pox victims? I've heard that will kill the lot of them. It won't waste ammunition, either. Certainly it's more tidy than bullets."

"I believe, sir, that such a shipment would be a long time coming. Major Gladwin is requesting immediate assistance and reinforcements."

"Very well than, he shall have it. I trust you can handle the assignment Captain Dalyell?"

Dalyell smiled smuggly as he marched up the river toward Pontiac's camp. He and his 260 soldiers had reached Major Gladwin at Fort Detroit thanks to a bank of thick fog which concealed them from the Indian villages on either side of the river.

This July night he was on his way to attack Pontiac's camp while the Indians slept. Surely it would be simple to wipe out these savages, he thought to himself as he and the first troops began to cross a narrow wooden bridge over a creek.

The quiet of the night was split by flashes of gun fire. The sound of shots and war whoops filled the air. Dalyell froze in shock. He saw his soldiers fall to the bridge deck, clutching their wounds. He nearly cried out in terror as all around him the night belched fire.

Dalyell dropped to the deck of the bridge and began to fire blindly into the darkened brush. They were surrounded, he soon discovered. Their only means of escape was blocked by war-crazed Indians.

For nearly an hour, Dalyell and his soldiers fired, reloaded and fired again. They rarely saw their enemies. Finally, Dalyell decided a charge was necessary to clear a route back to the fort. He jumped to his feet and gave the yell to retreat. Then he raced blindly toward the unseen foe.

A bullet ripped through his thigh as he ran, but Dalyell barely noticed it as he clawed his way back along the bridge.

"We must clear the road to the fort!" he screamed. Dropping to the ground, he hid in the brush to take stock of the situation. He scanned the dark horizon for a route of escape, but noted the only one was under fire from a band of Indians hiding in the foundation of an unfinished house.

"Charge!" he bellowed as he ran full into the blazing fire. Once he got his hands on the savages he would end the battle once and for all, he told himself as his feet pounded the damp forest floor. No Indian could defeat His Majesty's soldiers! No Indian could . . .

A tongue of fire licked his stomach, spreading quickly to his chest. He stumbled, grabbing for his belly to put out the fire. But it wouldn't leave, and it burned until he finally lay still and the noise of the battle faded into darkness.

Pontiac was silent as he surv scene. Dalyell's fatal charge h Indians, and the surviving sol mile back to the fort. Still, the who had not made it and nev blood had turned the water o dull crimson. From then on, i Bloody Run.

The war chief smiled to himse wearily back to camp. It had l But their victory had shown t supported them in their effort the English soldiers. Now, if o down Fort Detroit. Then their assured. The land would be s French.

Pontiac decided Fort Niagara target. Its location at the mout River and its role as a supplier made it ripe for an attack in th

Dalyell smiled smuggly as he marched up the river toward Pontiac's camp. He and his 260 soldiers had reached Major Gladwin at Fort Detroit thanks to a bank of thick fog which concealed them from the Indian villages on either side of the river.

This July night he was on his way to attack Pontiac's camp while the Indians slept. Surely it would be simple to wipe out these savages, he thought to himself as he and the first troops began to cross a narrow wooden bridge over a creek.

The quiet of the night was split by flashes of gun fire. The sound of shots and war whoops filled the air. Dalyell froze in shock. He saw his soldiers fall to the bridge deck, clutching their wounds. He nearly cried out in terror as all around him the night belched fire.

Dalyell dropped to the deck of the bridge and began to fire blindly into the darkened brush. They were surrounded, he soon discovered. Their only means of escape was blocked by war-crazed Indians.

For nearly an hour, Dalyell and his soldiers fired, reloaded and fired again. They rarely saw their enemies. Finally, Dalyell decided a charge was necessary to clear a route back to the fort. He jumped to his feet and gave the yell to retreat. Then he raced blindly toward the unseen foe.

A bullet ripped through his thigh as he ran, but Dalyell barely noticed it as he clawed his way back along the bridge.

"We must clear the road to the fort!" he screamed. Dropping to the ground, he hid in the brush to take stock of the situation. He scanned the dark horizon for a route of escape, but noted the only one was under fire from a band of Indians hiding in the foundation of an unfinished house.

"Charge!" he bellowed as he ran full into the blazing fire. Once he got his hands on the savages he would end the battle once and for all, he told himself as his feet pounded the damp forest floor. No Indian could defeat His Majesty's soldiers! No Indian could . . .

A tongue of fire licked his stomach, spreading quickly to his chest. He stumbled, grabbing for his belly to put out the fire. But it wouldn't leave, and it burned until he finally lay still and the noise of the battle faded into darkness.

Pontiac was silent as he surveyed the battle scene. Dalyell's fatal charge had dislodged the Indians, and the surviving soldiers had fled the mile back to the fort. Still, there were 20 soldiers who had not made it and never would. Their blood had turned the water of the creek into a dull crimson. From then on, it would be known as Bloody Run.

The war chief smiled to himself as he walked wearily back to camp. It had been a fierce battle. But their victory had shown that Manitou supported them in their efforts to rid the forest of the English soldiers. Now, if only they could bring down Fort Detroit. Then their victory would be assured. The land would be safe for them and the French.

Pontiac decided Fort Niagara would be the next target. Its location at the mouth of the Niagara River and its role as a supplier to Fort Detroit made it ripe for an attack in the fall.

Pontiac and his men were assembled around Niagara Falls, patiently awaiting the next boat of English supplies from the East. Once the supplies were unloaded, the English would haul them up from the falls on a narrow, rocky road. At the top, they would be reloaded into boats and taken to the fort. The narrow road would be the perfect place to attack.

Pontiac heard the sound of the white man hauling their supplies. They were coming up the narrow, twisting road. He motioned to his warriors to wait. He wanted the soldiers to be in the right spot before he attacked. The Indians were hiding in the woods. Pontiac waited for the soldiers to come between the woods and a steep cliff overlooking the falls.

The attack began as the soldiers reached the Indians' hiding place. With a wild cry, the Indians poured forth from the woods, guns flaring and tomahawks flashing. The soldiers' horses and oxen bellowed in panic and plunged over the cliffs taking soldiers with them to their deaths.

Pontiac looks over Niagara Falls.

With no retreat for the soldiers, the battle lasted only minutes. Of more than 80 British soldiers, only a handful survived. The rest lay battered and bloody along the narrow road, or, dashed to bits on the rocks of the mighty Niagara.

Despite the victory at Niagara Falls, Pontiac's Indian forces began to tire of the war. Winter was coming, and they had had no time to hunt and store up food for the cold days ahead. Slowly the warriors began to go back home, trading their guns for bows and arrows.

Pontiac tried with all his might to stir them to battle but to no avail. Finally, he realized that without help from the French, his war would end in his defeat.

October brought the first snow of the season. That day a French officer brought Pontiac a letter from the commander of Fort De Chartres, located in present-day Illinois. The war between France and England was over, the letter said, and the commander wished that Pontiac and his army lay down their arms as well. The aging chief sat down to write a letter to the commander.

My Brother, he wrote, *the word which my father has sent me to make peace I have accepted; all my young men have buried their hatchets.*

Pontiac's war was over.

Pontiac stepped out of the store at the French settlement of Cahokia. It was nearly three years after the war had ended. There had been three years of negotiations and shattered dreams. And now, he had been exiled to Illinois. Only a few friends and relatives had joined him there. Many of his people believed he had turned into a friend of the British. They thought that because he had negotiated with the British for his people's hunting rights.

As Pontiac went outside, he noticed someone following him. He saw that it was a Peoria Indian.

Pontiac took several steps down the street before he felt the crack of a club on his head. The elderly Pontiac tumbled to the ground, his eyes wide in amazement. The Peoria stood over him for an instant. The attacker fell upon him, stabbing him with a hunting knife.

The war chief who had united 18 powerful tribes against the mighty British was dead within minutes, killed by one of his own.